Anna Mae's

MAC N CHEESE

10 9 8 7 6 5 4 3 2 1

Square Peg, an imprint of Vintage,
20 Vauxhall Bridge Road,
London SW1V 2SA

Square Peg is part of the Penguin Random House
group of companies whose addresses can be found
at global.penguinrandomhouse.com.

Penguin
Random House
UK

Design by Friederike Huber
Photography by Fox & Favour
Styling by Laura Fyfe
Doodles by Annalee Soskin

Thanks to Sara Lincoln for kind permission to use her
photograph on page 4.

Every effort has been made to contact the subjects
of the photography, please contact the publisher
with any omissions.

First published by Square Peg in 2015

www.vintage-books.co.uk

A CIP catalogue record for this book is available
from the British Library

ISBN 9780224101219

Printed and bound by Replika Press Pvt. Ltd.

Penguin Random House is committed to a
sustainable future for our business, our readers
and our planet. This book is made from Forest
Stewardship Council® certified paper.

FSC
www.fsc.org
MIX
Paper from
responsible sources
FSC® C023419

Anna Mae's
MAC N CHEESE

**RECIPES FROM
LONDON'S LEGENDARY STREET FOOD TRUCK**

ANNA CLARK N TONY SOLOMON

◲ SQUARE PEG

CONTENTS

Our recipes

#Cheesuslovesyou
The Don Macaroni
Date Night
The Spicy Juan
My Big Mac Greek Wedding
Professor Green
Macgic Mushroom
Fight Club
The Macshugganer
Smokey and the Bandit
Mackney Wick
Bloody Mac
Lil' Kimchi
Glastonbrie
Mac Tribute
Maclette
Mac & Blue
Machos
Hot Chick
LL Cow J
Trailer Park Pie
RIP Sebastian
Fuck Yoga
MacDMA
Mac 'N' Sleaze
The Quick One
Mac No Cheese
Mac 'N' Cheese Fries
Superfry Snack Mac
Pasta Pat's Empanadas
The Smoke Choke Sourdough Press

Mac-Packed Peppers
Waffle Mac
Mac Boy Slim
Baby Cheesus
Scooby Macs
Charred Padron Peppers
Kwik Kimchi
Pickled Reds
Speedy Sauerkraut
Salsa Fresca
Guac'
Porno Pepper Sauce
Lemon-Dresses Spinach & Fennel
Avo & Butter Lettuce Salad
Roasted Brussels with
  Bacon Vinaigrette
Zena's Fried Cauliflower
  & Chard Salad
House Chilli

Pop Bitch
Deep-fried Ice Cream
Buttermilk Pancakes
In Transit
Strawberry Harshmellow Shake
The Green Man
Black Cherry Margaritas
GG&T
Buttered Coffee
A word about wine

SETTING OUT

TIPS · STARTER SAUCE · CHEESE

'MacCheese? What the hell is MacCheese?' – Anna's mum

HOW DID WE END UP WITH A RECIPE BOOK FULL OF MAC 'N' CHEESE RECIPES?

It was summer 2010 when it started, this street food adventure. We were both sick of our jobs, the routine, the samey-samey days – something needed to happen or we would go crazy. We both had ideas about what we could do next, but needed a starting point.

And then we found one. We both loved food – cooking it, eating it, finding it and talking about it. We were obsessed with markets we'd visited around the world and the stuff we ate from paper plates in car parks or on roadsides. Our favourite thing was the Southern food we discovered during trips to the United States which, with one or two exceptions, you couldn't find in the UK at the time.

We didn't have a plan, or any idea how we'd manage to earn a living from it, but we could feel the potential. So we jacked in our jobs and set off to LA, from where we headed south on a big-ass 5,000-mile road trip to research our idea… and eat shit-tons of food. Our parents and friends thought we were nuts and, to be fair, we weren't totally sure they weren't right.

SOUTHERN-FOOD SLUTS

When we got back to London we jumped in feet first and found a pitch at an underground market in a back garden in Kilburn, laying out £200 on a table, a couple of burners and some ingredients. Pulled pork was on the menu and no one had a clue what it was ('pulled??!') but, despite this, it sold well and we put the money made and the lessons learnt straight into our next event. We've never been lucky enough to have been handed a load of money so everything we have now – equipment, pitches, new stalls, the truck – has grown out of that initial investment. The philosophy of Anna Mae's has always been to constantly reinvest what we've made so that we can improve and make things even better.

We began to spread the Southern-food love through the streets of London, at first with our Notorious P.I.G pulled-pork

sandwiches, home-made BBQ sauce (still doin' it!) and sweetheart sesame slaw. We had a crack at cooking up everything from brisket, hushpuppies, Texas red chilli, chipotle-and-bourbon-spiked beans to cornbread and even rice pudding (maybe our friends were right!).

WHY JUST MAC 'N' CHEESE?

We get asked this all the time; it started on one of those days when everything goes wrong. It was pissing with rain and the van we'd hired had broken down so we had no choice but to decide what equipment and food we could carry for the last leg of the journey to our pitch. We both went for the mac 'n' cheese. We hadn't realised it until then, but it was the one dish among all the others that we loved the most. Mac 'n' cheese was our lobster.

Whether it was that American staple Kraft mac in a box, or a poncey black-truffle number, posh or not, mac 'n' cheese had always got us in our gut. It's infused with a primal pull that leaves us satisfied but forever looking for our next cheesy hit.

We weren't sure if anyone else shared this hunger for the mac goodness, so setting up the stall was a little more nerve-wracking than usual that day. But they did. We sold out and had our best day's trading ever. It was a moment that changed our lives and we decided then and there to devote our future to mac 'n' cheese street-slinging.

We were excited: we knew we were on to something special. The initial buzz from Twitter was huge. No one else was specialising in mac 'n' cheese. The next six months was a whirlwind of ingredient, pasta and cheese trials, and experiments with flavour combinations.

Since that rainy day four years ago we've not looked back. The queues keep forming and the accolades keep coming: it's been a trip. And now we make the best mac 'n' cheese in London.

THE MAC LIFE

We've cooked everywhere from the London 2012 Olympics and red-carpet premieres to a muddy field in Somerset; for tiny wedding parties in Dorset to massive corporations like Nike, Converse and Google. We've won awards, appeared on the telly and been raved about by journalists. We've built stalls and watched them collapse; argued like crazy, then kissed and made up; worked all night, danced all night, drowned our sorrows and downed pints. We've held up gazebos in the rain and weighted down gazebos in the wind; wished we were back in our office jobs and wished we'd given them up sooner; made many mistakes; learnt many lessons; met some of our best friends and realised who our real mates are. We've cut our fingers, burnt some flesh and sweated buckets; cried because we were exhausted, but mostly cried because we were happy.

We wouldn't change a thing.

Every recipe in this book is a result of all the things that have happened along the way.

TIPS

THE RECIPES IN THIS BOOK ARE
INTENDED AS A GUIDE. MAC 'N' CHEESE
ISN'T A COMPLICATED DISH AND
COOKING IT SHOULD BE FUN AND EASY,
SO LET'S NOT GET POLITICAL – USE OUR
IDEAS AS INSPIRATION AND MIX THINGS
UP AS YOU WISH.

Use elbow macaroni or don't;
spend a bomb on fancy fromage or
just use the supermarket stuff;
do it stove-top with crispy panko
or grilled with a crust - it's up
to you.

We do have one golden rule: use loads of cheese. If you're not sure it's enough, it's not – add more.

HERE ARE A FEW THINGS TO KEEP IN MIND TO MAKE SURE YOU'RE ON TO A WINNER WHEN THAT FORKFUL HITS THE FIFTH SENSE:

WE USE ELBOW MACARONI but good alternatives are chifferi, orecciette, penne, rigatoni, just make sure whatever you use has a high percentage of durum semolina (you'll know because the pasta will have a golden colour) and is nice and thickly cut so that it holds its shape when it's fully cooked. Cheese sauce clings to curly, hollow shapes the best.

SEASON WITH THE STUFF FROM THE SEA, not iodised table salt which can leave a metallic taste.

ALWAYS DRAIN THE PASTA as best you can – too much water can make the cheese sauce go weird. Don't add any oil when you boil the pasta either – it will also mess with the sauce.

TAKE THE PASTA OFF THE HEAT when it's still slightly undercooked (al dente) as it will continue to cook while it drains and when it's added to the sauce.

INVEST in a heavy-bottomed saucepan: it evenly distributes the heat and means there's less chance of burning the sauce.

BETTER TO KEEP THE HEAT LOW rather than high – if anything starts to curdle, high heat is probably the reason why.

CHEESE GRATES A LOT MORE EASILY when it's cold and melts a lot more easily when it's grated finely, so make life easier and stick the cheese in the fridge before grating and use the fine shred on your grater.

THE THICKNESS OF YOUR SAUCE will vary according to the type of cheese you use, and may even depend on the producer and the batch. If your sauce is too runny or not cheesy enough just add more cheese.

ALL RECIPES SERVE 4 unless stated otherwise.

STARTER SAUCE

**THERE ARE TWO STAGES TO MAKING A
GOOD CHEESE SAUCE: MAKING THE
BASE, AND ADDING THE CHEESE. THIS
RECIPE WILL GIVE YOU THE BASE FOR ALL
THE MAC RECIPES IN THIS BOOK; JUST
ADD WHATEVER CHEESE THE RECIPE
REQUIRES, OR GO FREESTYLE.**

Makes 1 portion

600ml whole milk, at room
  temperature
50g unsalted butter
50g plain flour
a pinch of salt

Place two heavy-bottomed pans
over a medium heat.

Heat the milk in one pan until
hot, but not boiling.

At the same time melt the butter
in the second pan, then reduce
the heat to low and gradually
stir in the flour using a wooden
spoon until you have a paste
- this is a roux. Continue to
cook, stirring continuously, for
3-4 minutes, or until the roux
turns golden in colour, being
careful not to overbrown and
burn the mixture.

Add the hot milk to the roux
a little at a time, stirring
vigorously. Once the mixture
is fully combined, turn up the
heat to medium and cook for a
further 5-8 minutes, or until
the sauce is thick enough to
coat the back of the wooden
spoon. Make sure you stir
continuously to keep the sauce
smooth and so that it doesn't
stick to the bottom of the pan.
Season with salt.

CHEESE

CHEDDAR
COW • UK • HARD

Mac benefits: Cheddar - the cheese we all know and love. It's the classic cheesy flavour and grandpappy of a good cheese sauce. Think of cheese toasties round your friend's house as a kid; chunks eaten straight from the fridge when you're hung over; that whiff of your granddad's oily shed that hits the nostrils before the first bite.

MONTEREY JACK
COW • US • SEMI-HARD

Mac benefits: Jack is a bit of a slut - its versatile, mild flavour goes with everything. It also gives a cool kinda creaminess that allows other flavours to bust through.

MOZZARELLA
COW/BUFFALO • ITA • SEMI-SOFT

Mac benefits: Not just a pizza topping adored by Ninja Turtles, this creamy ball of niceness lends a milkiness to any dish, plus that stringy cheesy awesomeness that sticks to your chin.

HAVARTI
COW • DMK • SEMI-SOFT

Mac benefits: The Danes aren't just responsible for great pastries, LEGO™ (who knew?) and supermodels: they also make a very tasty cheese. Havarti adds a salty bite that works super well with sweeter or pickled toppings.

BRIE
COW • FRA • SOFT

Mac benefits: The common-sense reaction to something covered in a smelly mould is to get rid, but remove its little jacket and the deliciously soft centre will give you a super creamy mac.

GRUYÈRE
COW • SWI • HARD

Mac benefits: Nuttier than a squirrel's nutsack. Gives your mac a - you guessed it - nutty depth that sends people… nuts. Love this stuff.

PARMESAN
COW • ITA • HARD

Mac benefits: If you want to ramp up the umami of any dish, this is your guy: it's strong, sharp, nutty and fruity and will put the cheese in your mac 'n' cheese. The reason it goes great with Parma ham? Leftover whey from the cheese is used to feed the pigs that Parma ham comes from. Love a good fact.

PROVOLONE
COW • ITA • SEMI-HARD

Mac benefits: Gives good depth of flavour and smoothness. Add the dolce variety for a touch of sweetness.

TALEGGIO
COW • ITA • SEMI-SOFT

Mac benefits: This Italian stallion of a cheese makes us go weak at the knees. Brings a delicious fruitiness to your mac, and goes spectacularly well with mushrooms.

MUNSTER
COW • FRA • SOFT

Mac benefits: It tastes great but boy does it stink. Satisfying any cheese lover's need for intense cheesiness, this adds a strong and savoury element to your mac 'n' cheese, but also a hint of sweetness.

STILTON
COW • UK • SEMI-SOFT & CRUMBLY

Mac benefits: Makes it taste like Stilton, lil' stupid.

DEAR Mac +
Cheese

You make
the best
mac + cheese
Ever!!

Mac and Cheesey Thoughts.
By: Cubs The Poet.

Melting memories,

    held together by

    cheddar.

Love is like a wet noodle,
  soaking up all the tears

    we wasted on
      while cooking
  boiling water.

Cheese has way of creating
  an aroma of
    love.
Lets add alittle more.

These plain shells, are selfish
  only the
    ones with
    enough
      time can last
  in a wworld of side dishes
our entree of cheesy thoughts
have evolved into a main
  dish of happiness.

1.23.15

FROM THE TRUCK

OUR CLASSIC MAC RECIPES

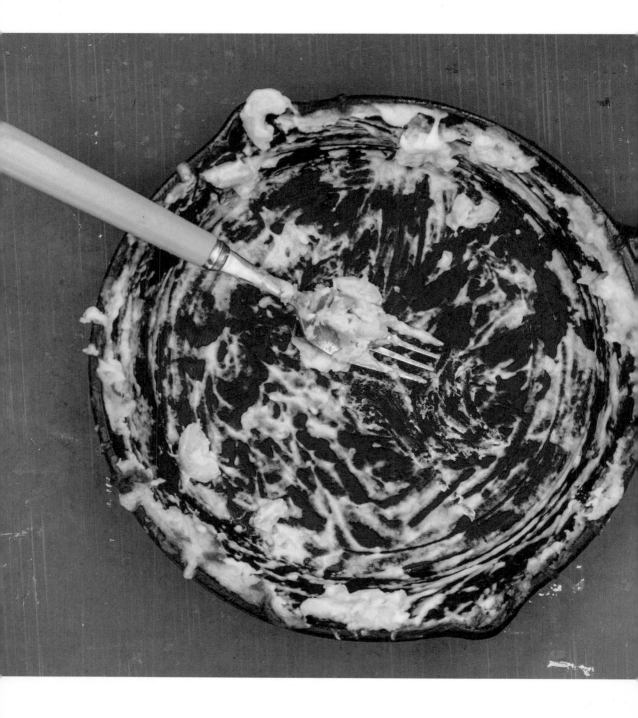

#CHEESUSLOVESYOU

THIS IS THE RECIPE THAT STARTED US ON OUR MAC 'N' CHEESE PILGRIMAGE.

400g macaroni
1 x portion Starter Sauce
  (page 21)
230g mature Cheddar, grated
90g Monterey Jack, grated
30g Parmesan, grated
½ tsp English mustard
30g mozzarella, grated

Preheat the grill to 220°C/200°C (fan)/gas 7.

Bring a large pan of salted water to the boil and cook the pasta according to the pack instructions, until al dente. Tip into a colander and leave to drain completely.

In a heavy-bottomed pan, make the Starter Sauce, then reduce the heat to low. Add all the cheese except the mozzarella, then the mustard, and stir until melted. Stir in the drained pasta.

Transfer the mixture to an ovenproof dish, sprinkle over the mozzarella and place under the grill for 6-8 minutes, or until blistered and bubbling. Woof.

THE DON MACARONI

THIS IS THE MOST POPULAR DISH WE SELL OUT OF THE TRUCK – PEOPLE GO CRAZY FOR BACON. HERE WE'RE USING THE FAT FROM THE PAN TO CREATE EVEN BIGGER BACON FLAVOUR.

400g macaroni
1 x portion Starter Sauce
  (page 21)
230g mature Cheddar, grated
90g Monterey Jack, grated
30g Parmesan, grated
8 rashers of dry-cured streaky
  bacon
freshly ground black pepper

FOR THE PESTO
75ml good-quality olive oil
25g grated Parmesan
25g pine nuts
1 garlic clove
10 fresh basil leaves, plus
  extra to garnish
a squeeze of lemon

First make the pesto. Pop the ingredients into a small bowl and blitz with a hand blender, or bash in a pestle and mortar until lovely and smooth. Set aside.

Bring a large pan of salted water to the boil and cook the pasta according to the pack instructions, until al dente. Tip into a colander and leave to drain completely.

In a heavy-bottomed pan make the Starter Sauce, then reduce the heat to low. Stir in all the cheese and leave to melt, stirring occasionally to stop the mixture sticking to the pan. Add the drained pasta to the cheese sauce and mix thoroughly.

Meanwhile, fry the bacon until crisp, pouring any fat that collects in the pan into the cheese sauce, mixing well.

Spoon the mac 'n' cheese into 4 serving bowls, drizzle the pesto over the top and place two of the bacon rashers across each dish. Garnish with the basil and season with freshly ground pepper.

DATE NIGHT

GARLIC AND CHEESE IS A CLASSIC COMBO – WHO CARES ABOUT GARLIC BREATH. YOU COULD USE SMOKED GARLIC FOR A REAL DEPTH OF FLAVOUR, BUT MAYBE HAVE A FEW CHEEKY TIC-TACS HANDY.

whole head of garlic
tbsp olive oil
tbsp unsalted butter
g Japanese panko breadcrumbs
)g macaroni
:bsp milk
portion Starter Sauce
(page 21)
190g Gruyère, grated
100g Monterey Jack, grated
30g Parmesan, grated
1 tsp finely chopped fresh
oregano leaves

Preheat the oven to 240°C/180°C (fan)/gas 6.

First roast the garlic. Chop the top off the bulb to expose the tops of the cloves inside. Drizzle with the olive oil and wrap the bulb in tin foil. Bake for 30 minutes, or until soft and caramelised.

Meanwhile, melt the butter in a frying pan over a low heat and toss in the panko breadcrumbs to coat. Increase the heat to medium and toast the breadcrumbs until golden. Set aside.

Bring a large pan of salted water to the boil and cook the pasta according to the pack instructions, until al dente. Tip into a colander and leave to drain completely.

Once the garlic head is cooked through, remove from the oven. Carefully separate the cloves from the bulb and squeeze the flesh from the skins into a small bowl. Add the milk. Using a hand blender or pestle and mortar, blitz or bash until smooth.

In a heavy-bottomed pan make the Starter Sauce, then reduce the heat to low and add the cheeses and garlic paste. Stir until the cheese has melted, then stir in the drained pasta.

Transfer the mac 'n' cheese to a serving dish and sprinkle with the toasted panko breadcrumbs and oregano.

THE SPICY JUAN

THIS IS OUR MOST POPULAR VEGGIE OPTION, WITH A DEDICATED FAN BASE WHO HAVE RECREATED IT AT HOME. WE'VE CHANGED A FEW THINGS HERE, BUT IT'S STILL THE VEGGIES' FAVOURITE JUAN.

400g macaroni
1 x portion Starter Sauce
  (page 21)
230g mature Cheddar, grated
90g queso Chihuahua
  (or Monterey Jack), grated
30g Parmesan, grated
4 tsp chipotle paste
  (or to taste)
1 x jar red jalapeño chilies,
  or a couple of chopped, fresh
  chilies
a handful of fresh coriander
  leaves
4 tbsp soured cream, to serve

Bring a large pan of salted water to the boil and cook the pasta according to the pack instructions, until al dente. Tip into a colander and leave to drain completely.

Meanwhile, in a heavy-bottomed pan make the Starter Sauce, then reduce the heat to low. Add all the cheese and stir until melted. Add the drained pasta and chipotle paste and stir through.

Spoon the mac into 4 bowls and top with as many jalapeños as you like, and a good pinch of fresh coriander. Serve the soured cream in a bowl so that people can help themselves should you go a bit nuts with the heat.

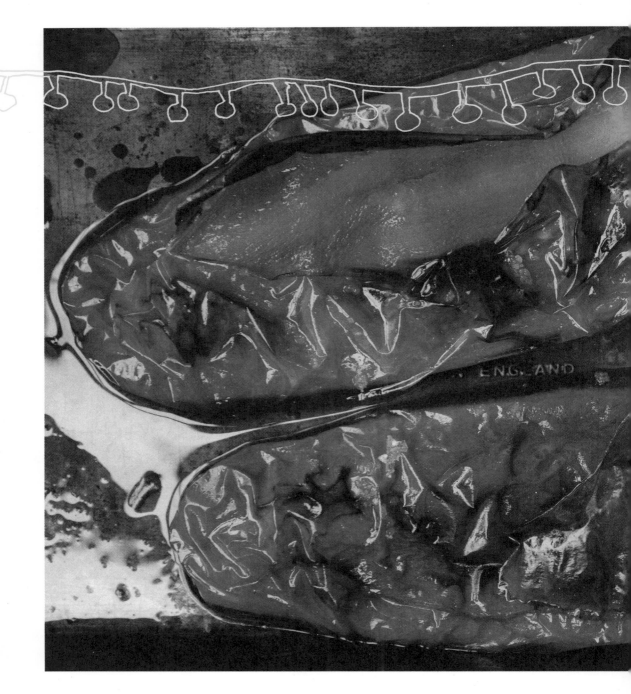

MY BIG MAC GREEK WEDDING

THESE FLAVOURS ARE A PERFECT MATCH.

2 medium-sized pointed red
  peppers, seeded
400g macaroni
1 x portion Starter Sauce
  (page 21)
230g mature Cheddar, grated
90g Monterey Jack, grated
30g Parmesan, grated
80g Kalamata olives, pitted and
  sliced thinly
120g feta, crumbled
a good pinch of chopped fresh
  Greek basil
freshly ground black pepper

Preheat the oven to 200°C/180°C
(fan)/gas 6.

Place the seeded peppers on
a baking tray and bake for
30 minutes, or until the skin
is nice and charred. Remove
from the oven and slice into
rounds 1cm thick. Switch your
oven setting to grill.

While the peppers are roasting,
bring a large pan of salted
water to the boil and cook the
pasta according to the pack
instructions, until al dente.
Tip into a colander and leave
to drain completely.

In a heavy-bottomed pan make
the Starter Sauce, then reduce
the heat to low and add all the
cheese except the feta. Stir
until melted, then add the olive
and pepper slices and mix.

Stir in the drained pasta then
transfer the lot to an ovenproof
dish and sprinkle over the feta.
Grill for 5 minutes or until the
feta has softened. Season with
pepper and garnish with the
fresh Greek basil for final
beautification.

PROFESSOR GREEN

WE CREATED THIS MAC FOR A PROFESSOR GREEN GIG WE DID A WHILE AGO. HOW COULD WE HAVE KNOWN THE GUY HATES CHEESE?

6 rashers streaky bacon, sliced
  into thin pieces
400g macaroni
1 x portion Starter Sauce
  (page 21)
230g mature Cheddar, grated
90g Monterey Jack, grated
8 tbsp Guac' (page 111)
4 large free-range eggs
a pinch of smoked paprika
1 bunch fresh chives, finely
  chopped
olive oil, for frying

Cook the bacon in a frying pan over a medium-high heat until brown and crisp. Remove from the pan, reserving the fat, and pat dry with kitchen paper. Set aside.

Bring a large pan of salted water to the boil and cook the pasta according to the pack instructions, until al dente. Tip into a colander and leave to drain completely.

In a heavy-bottomed pan, make the Starter Sauce, then reduce the heat to low. Add all the cheese and stir until melted. Add the guacamole, stir through, then add the drained pasta and mix well.

Reheat the pan with the bacon fat to medium and fry the eggs until the white is firm but the yolk is runny.

Divide the guac-mac mixture into 4 bowls, lay an egg on each one then scatter over the bacon pieces. Dust each yolk with paprika and garnish with the chopped chives.

MACGIC MUSHROOM

**WE WENT HUNTING FOR MUSHROOMS
IN THE WOODS AT WILDERNESS FESTIVAL:
WE DIDN'T' FIND ANY – IT WAS AUGUST.**

400g macaroni
1 x portion Starter Sauce
  (page 21)
150g mild Cheddar, grated
120g taleggio, rind removed and
  cheese cubed
30g Parmesan, finely grated
a drizzle of black truffle oil
a small handful of fresh sage
  leaves, finely chopped

FOR THE MUSHROOM RAGOUT
a large knob of butter
3 shallots
2 garlic cloves, crushed
3 fresh thyme sprigs, leaves
  picked
250g chestnut mushrooms,
  chopped
250g field mushrooms, chopped
250ml dry white wine

sea salt and freshly ground
  pepper

Preheat the grill to 220°C/200°C
(fan)/gas 7.

First make the mushroom ragout.
In a sauté pan over a medium
heat, melt the butter, then add
the shallots, garlic and thyme
leaves and cook until softened.
Add the chopped mushrooms and
stir, then add the wine. Add a
pinch each of salt and pepper
and leave to reduce on the heat
until the liquid has thickened
but not disappeared.

Bring a large pan of salted
water to the boil and cook the
pasta according to the pack
instructions, until al dente.
Tip into a colander and leave
to drain completely.

In a heavy-bottomed pan make
the Starter Sauce, then reduce
the heat to low. Add the
Cheddar and talegio and stir
until melted. Stir in the
drained pasta.

Grab an ovenproof dish and pour in half the mac, then evenly spoon over all the mushroom ragout. Pour the rest of your mac over the 'shrooms, sandwiching them in the centre. Sprinkle the grated Parmesan over the top and place under the grill for 10 minutes, or until golden.

Remove from the grill and drizzle with the truffle oil, bearing in mind that that shit is strong. Sprinkle over some chopped sage and serve at the table for maximum truffly impressiveness.

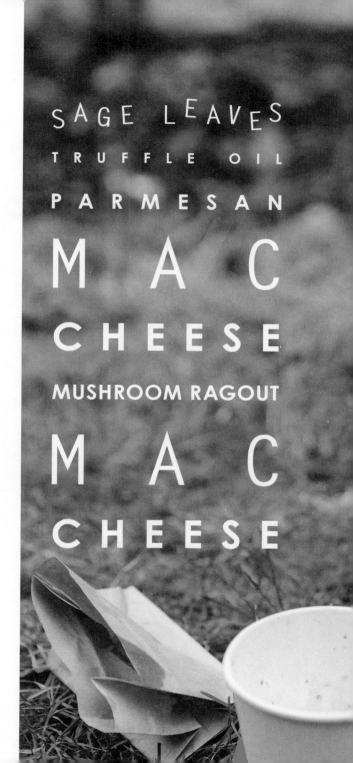

SAGE LEAVES

TRUFFLE OIL

PARMESAN

MAC

CHEESE

MUSHROOM RAGOUT

MAC

CHEESE

This mac is packed with punchy umami.

FIGHT CLUB

300g salsiccia (about
  4 sausages), skin removed
400g macaroni
8 spears tenderstem broccoli,
  cut into 3cm pieces
1 x portion Starter Sauce
  (page 21)
230g Double Gloucester, grated
90g Fontina, grated
30g Parmesan, grated
140g Taleggio, rind removed
  and cheese sliced
1 tsp dried chilli flakes

Preheat the grill to 200°C/180°C
(fan)/gas 6.

Place a sauté pan over a medium
heat. Roll the sausage meat into
balls roughly 3cm wide and
transfer to the pan, then fry
for about 8 minutes, or until
cooked through.

Bring a large pan of salted
water to the boil and cook the
pasta according to the pack
instructions, until al dente.
Tip into a colander and leave
to drain completely.

Meanwhile, bring another pan
of salted water to the boil
and blanch the broccoli for
1 minute, drain and pat
completely dry with kitchen
paper.

In a heavy-bottomed pan make
the Starter Sauce, then reduce
the heat to low. Add the Double
Gloucester, fontina and Parmesan
and stir until melted. Add the
sausage meat, blanched broccoli
and drained pasta to the sauce
and mix well.

Transfer the mac 'n' cheese to
an ovenproof dish and top with
the sliced taleggio. Pop under
the grill for 10 minutes, or
until the taleggio is melted.
Sprinkle with the chilli flakes
and get stuck in.

THE MACSHUGGANER

THIS IS A RECIPE INSPIRED BY OUR JEWISH-DELI SANDWICH OBSESSION. *MESHUGGAH* **JUST HAPPENS TO MEANS 'CRAZY' IN YIDDISH, WHICH IS WHAT PEOPLE CALLED US WHEN WE PACKED IN OUR JOBS TO DEVOTE OUR LIVES TO MAC 'N' CHEESE.**

400g macaroni
1 x portion Starter Sauce
   (page 21)
230g mature Cheddar, grated
90g Monterey Jack, grated
30g Parmesan, grated
½ tsp American mustard
8 thin slices pastrami
4 slices Emmental
4 tbsp Speedy Sauerkraut
   (page 110)
4 small pinches of chopped
   fresh dill

Bring a large pan of salted water to the boil and cook the pasta according to the pack instructions, until al dente. Tip into a colander and leave to drain completely.

In a heavy-bottomed pan make the Starter Sauce, then reduce the heat to low. Add the Cheddar, Monterey Jack, Parmesan and mustard and stir until melted. Stir in the drained pasta.

Spoon the mac 'n' cheese into 4 serving bowls, and layer 2 slices of pastrami followed by a slice of Emmental over each dish. Blowtorch the cheese until melted and bubbling. (Alternatively transfer the mac to an ovenproof dish, top with the pastrami and cheese and pop under the grill for a few minutes until melted.)

Serve each mac with a dollop of sauerkraut and a pinch of dill.

Es gezunterheyt!

SMOKEY AND THE BANDIT

WE FIRST MET OUR TRUCK ON A DRIVEWAY IN CROYDON, SOUTH LONDON. IT WAS A GREY DAY IN JANUARY.

HE DIDN'T LOOK MUCH; A GMC VENDOR FROM '86 WITH A CHIPPED GREY PAINT JOB AND SOME PERVY BUMPER STICKERS WRITTEN IN GERMAN ON HIS REAR DOORS. EACH OF HIS TYRES WAS A DIFFERENT SIZE AND HIS BRAKES DIDN'T WORK, WHICH WE ONLY REALISED WHEN IT WAS TOO LATE (OUCH) – BUT SOMETHING TOLD US HE WAS THE ONE.

WE TOWED HIM AWAY, STRIPPED HIM NAKED AND RECHRISTENED HIM BURT REYNOLDS AFTER THE MOUSTACHIOED LEGEND OF THE SILVER SCREEN, LADIES' MAN AND DEFENDER OF THE GOOD WHILST WEARING EXCELLENT COWBOY BOOTS. IT SEEMED THE NATURAL NAME FOR THE MAC VAN OF OUR DREAMS.

THIS RECIPE IS FOR HIM.

400g macaroni
1 x portion Starter Sauce
  (page 21)
230g smoked Cheddar, grated
90g Monterey Jack, grated
1 portion Pickled Reds
  (page 110)

Bring a large pan of salted water to the boil and cook the pasta according to the pack instructions, until al dente. Tip into a colander and leave to drain completely.

In a heavy-bottomed pan, make the Starter Sauce, then reduce the heat to low. Add all the cheese and stir until melted. Add the drained pasta to the cheese sauce and mix thoroughly.

Divide into 4 bowls and serve with our Pickled Reds.

MACKNEY WICK

ANNA MAE'S WAS INSPIRED BY OUR TRAVELS AROUND THE STATES, BUT WE ARE LONDON THROUGH AND THROUGH. THIS RECIPE IS A NOD TO OUR HOMETOWN AND THE GOOD OLD TRADITIONAL LONDON PUB, OR 'THE OFFICE' AS WE CALL IT.

400g macaroni
1 x portion Starter Sauce
   (page 21)
80ml Indian Pale Ale
230g mature Cheddar, grated
90g Monterey Jack, grated
30g Parmesan, grated
½ tsp English mustard
a handful of finely chopped
   fresh chives

FOR THE PORK SCRATCHINGS
500g pork rind with around
   1cm fat
2 tbsp sea salt, plus a pinch
1 tbsp celery salt
½ tsp smoked paprika

Prepare the pork scratchings. Pat dry the pork rind with kitchen paper. Rub the sea salt into the skin and chill in the fridge for at least an hour, but the longer the better.

Preheat the oven to 220°C/200°C (fan)/gas 7.

Take the chilled rind from the fridge, rub in the celery salt and cut into strips about 2cm long. Place on a wire rack over a roasting tray and roast for about 20 minutes, turning the tray every 5 minutes so that the skin doesn't burn. Remove from the oven when the skin is golden and crisp. Toss the scratchings in the paprika seasoned with a pinch of salt. Set aside.

Meanwhile, bring a large pan of salted water to the boil and cook the pasta according to the pack instructions, until al dente. Tip into a colander and leave to drain completely.

In a heavy-bottomed pan make the Starter Sauce, then reduce the heat to low. Gradually add the ale and stir through the sauce. Add the cheese and stir until melted, followed by the mustard and drained pasta. Drink any remaining beer.

Spoon the mac 'n' cheese into 4 bowls and top with the scratchings. Sprinkle over the fresh chives and serve.

BLOODY MAC

WE HAVE A VARIETY OF HANGOVER CURES AT ANNA MAE'S. THIS ONE IS DEDICATED TO CREW MEMBER ADAM, WHO SEEMS TO SUFFER MORE THAN MOST. SERVE IT WITH A SHOT OF VODKA, TO TAKE THE EDGE OFF.

250g cherry tomatoes, halved
2 tbsp Tabasco sauce, plus a
  few splashes
2 tbsp Worcestershire sauce
2 tbsp olive oil
400g macaroni
1 x portion Starter Sauce
  (page 21)
230g mature Cheddar, grated
90g Monterey Jack, grated
30g Parmesan, grated
sea salt and freshly ground
  black pepper
2 sticks celery, cut in half and
  sliced lengthways, to serve

First make the topping. Pop the tomatoes into a small bowl along with the Tabasco, Worcestershire sauce and olive oil and mix gently so all the tomatoes are lightly coated. Season with salt and pepper and set aside.

Bring a large pan of salted water to the boil and cook the pasta according to the pack instructions, until al dente. Tip into a colander and leave to drain completely.

In a heavy-bottomed pan, make the Starter Sauce, then reduce the heat to low. Add all the cheese and stir until melted. Add the drained pasta to the cheese sauce and mix thoroughly.

Divide the mac 'n' cheese into 4 serving bowls. Spoon the tomatoes evenly over each one along with a little of the dressing from the bowl. Stand a couple of celery pieces in the mac and season with freshly ground pepper and Tabasco, to taste.

LIL' KIMCHI

BEING PART OF THE ROAMING BAND OF KERB TRADERS WE GET TO WORK WITH PEOPLE COOKING SOME OF THE BEST STREET FOOD AROUND, FROM WHOOPIE PIES TO FABULOUS DOSAS. ONE OF OUR FAVOURITE THINGS TO DO IS TO TRY OTHER TRADERS' LEFTOVERS WITH OUR MAC. SOMETIMES THE WEIRDEST FLAVOUR COMBOS ARE SURPRISINGLY AWESOME – WE GAVE KIMCHI A GO AFTER ONE EVENT AND THE RESULT WAS TOTALLY DELISH.

400g macaroni
1 x portion Starter Sauce
   (page 21)
125g Kwik Kimchi (page 109),
   fully drained and roughly
   chopped
5 tbsp gochugaru paste (Korean
   chilli paste)
150g mature Cheddar, grated
150g Havarti cheese, grated
3 green jalapeño chillies, sliced
a handful of coriander leaves
3 spring onions, finely sliced
a few pinches of smoked paprika

Bring a large pan of salted water to the boil and cook the pasta according to the pack instructions, until al dente. Tip into a colander and leave to drain completely.

In a heavy-bottomed pan, make the Starter Sauce, then reduce the heat to low. Add the kimchi, gochugaru paste and all the cheese and stir until melted. Stir in the drained pasta.

Transfer the mac 'n' cheese to 4 serving dishes and top with the jalapeños, coriander, spring onion and a few pinches of smoked paprika. Stuff your face like you're Kim Jong-un locked in a room with a block of cheese.

GLASTONBRIE

THIS PUN IS TOO GOOD TO MISS, JUST LIKE THE FESTIVAL THAT INSPIRED IT. MATCH IT WITH A CIDER COCKTAIL (PAGE 129) FOR THE FULL EXPERIENCE.

400g macaroni
1 tbsp unsalted butter
70g Japanese panko breadcrumbs
60g shop-bought or home-made
  crispy onions
1 x portion Starter Sauce
  (page 21)
150g mild Cheddar, grated
150g Somerset brie, rind removed
  and cheese cubed
a few sprigs of rosemary

Bring a large pan of salted water to the boil and cook the pasta according to the pack instructions, until al dente. Tip into a colander and leave to drain completely.

Melt the butter in a frying pan over a low heat and toss in the panko breadcrumbs to coat. Lower the heat to medium and toast the breadcrumbs until golden. Set aside. Crush the crispy onions and mix them with the toasted breadcrumbs. Set aside.

In a heavy-bottomed pan, make the Starter Sauce, then reduce the heat to low. Add all the cheese and stir until melted. Stir in the drained pasta.

Transfer to 4 serving bowls, cover with the panko breadcrumb mixture and beautify with sprigs of rosemary.

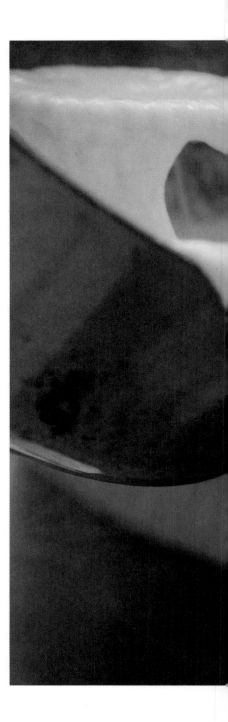

HOT TOPPINGS, FILTHY COMBOS

BRINGING SEXY MAC

MAC TRIBUTE

THIS IS OUR TRIBUTE TO AN AMERICAN CLASSIC. TASTES EXACTLY LIKE A BIG MAC® BURGER IN A BOWL, WEIRDED US RIGHT OUT.

400g macaroni
1 x portion Starter Sauce
  (page 21)
230g mature Cheddar, grated
90g Monterey Jack, grated
30g Parmesan, grated
350g beef mince
4 slices of burger cheese
1 onion, very finely diced
2 gherkins, sliced into rounds
½ iceberg lettuce, cut into
  fine strips
1 tbsp sesame seeds

FOR THE SAUCE
120g mayonnaise
2 tbsp finely chopped sweet
  gherkins
2 tsp American mustard
1 tsp white wine vinegar
1 tsp paprika
½ tsp garlic powder
½ tsp onion powder
a pinch of salt

In a small bowl, mix the ingredients for the sauce. Stick your finger in and taste - freaked out yet? Set aside.

Bring a large pan of salted water to the boil and cook the pasta until al dente. Tip into a colander and leave to drain completely.

In a heavy-bottomed pan, make the Starter Sauce, then reduce the heat to low. Add all the cheese and stir until melted. Stir in the drained pasta. Stir occasionally to stop sticking.

Meanwhile, grease a non-stick frying pan set over a medium heat. Roll the beef mince into 4 equal-sized balls and press down to make patties about 1cm thick. Fry until medium rare, about 2 minutes. Roughly break up into pieces.

Spoon the mac 'n' cheese into 4 bowls. Lay a slice of cheese over the top of each one. Divide the beef equally and sprinkle over each bowl, spoon over a little sauce and add the onion, gherkin and lettuce, in that order. Finish with a sprinkle of sesame seeds. You'll be transported right back to that service station on the M1 at 2 a.m., driving back from your mate's stag weekend.

MACLETTE

THIS DISH HAS PROPER BOLD WINTRY FLAVOURS THAT MAKE YOU WANT TO GO ALPINE AND HIT THE APRÈS SKI. RACLETTE IS A DISH WHERE EVERYONE CHOWS DOWN TOGETHER, WHICH IS ALSO THE BEST WAY TO ENJOY MAC 'N' CHEESE. SO, FIND A SUITABLY BIG DISH FOR YOUR MAC, POUR MOLTEN CHEESE OVER THE TOP STRAIGHT FROM THE PAN, AND GET STUCK IN.

400g macaroni
250g smoked bacon lardons
1 x portion Starter Sauce
  (page 21)
140g mild Cheddar, grated
120g Fontina, grated
200g Raclette, thickly sliced

TO SERVE
12 cornichons
a handful of pickled onions
2 tbsp wholegrain mustard

Bring a large pan of salted water to the boil and cook the pasta according to the pack instructions, until al dente. Tip into a colander and leave to drain completely.

Meanwhile, fry the bacon lardons in a frying pan over a medium heat until cooked through, remove and pat dry with kitchen paper.

In a heavy-bottomed pan, make the Starter Sauce, then reduce the heat to low. Add the Cheddar and Fontina and stir until melted. Add the drained pasta to the sauce along with the cooked lardons, stirring occasionally to stop it sticking.

Heat a non-stick frying pan over a medium-low flame and cook the Raclette slices until just melted.

Spoon the mac 'n' cheese into your serving dish and pour over the melted Raclette. Serve with cornichons, pickled onions and a few spoonfuls of mustard on the side. So alpine yo.

MAC & BLUE

THIS MIGHT JUST BE OUR DESERT-ISLAND DISH: MMMEEEEEEEEAT, MMMM CCCHHHHEEESE!

400g macaroni
1 x portion Starter Sauce
  (page 21)
200g mild Cheddar, grated
160g creamy blue cheese such
  as Colston Bassett Stilton
  (or Cambozola for the novice
  blue-cheese eater), crumbled
½ tsp Worcestershire sauce
4 x 250g rib-eye steaks
  (preferably dry-aged)
a handful of pea shoots
sea salt and freshly ground
  black pepper

Preheat a griddle to hot.

Bring a large pan of salted water to the boil and cook the pasta according to the pack instructions, until al dente. Tip into a colander and leave to drain completely.

In a heavy-bottomed pan, make the Starter Sauce, then reduce the heat to low. Add all the cheese and Worcestershire sauce and stir until melted. Stir in the drained pasta and stir occasionally to stop it sticking.

Generously salt the steaks, then cook on the hot griddle for 2 minutes each side, until medium rare. Remove from the heat and slice each steak diagonally across the grain of the meat into 4 or 5 strips.

Divide the mac 'n' cheese into 4 serving bowls, place the sliced steak over the top and finish with black pepper and the pea shoots.

MACHOS

THIS IS A FULLY PIMPED ANNA MAE'S
VERSION OF THAT ALL-TIME CLASSIC
SHARING DISH, NACHOS. YOUR MATES
WILL CONTINUOUSLY ASK YOU TO MAKE
IT WHEN THEY COME OVER TO WATCH
THE EUROVISION SONG CONTEST AND
THINK THAT BRINGING A 4-PACK MAKES
UP FOR ALL THE EFFORT YOU'VE PUT IN
TO LOVINGLY PREPARING THIS MOUTH-
WATERING FEAST. SORRY ABOUT THAT.

400g macaroni
1 x portion Starter Sauce
  (page 21)
230g mature Cheddar, grated
90g queso Chihuahua (or Monterey
  Jack), grated
30g Parmesan, grated
200g plain corn chips
1 x portion House Chilli
  (page 119)
4 tbsp Guac' (page 111)
4 tbsp Salsa Fresca (page 111)
1 x jar red jalapeño chillies
4 tbsp soured cream
a small bunch of coriander,
  leaves picked
2 limes, cut into quarters

Bring a large pan of salted
water to the boil and cook the
pasta according to the pack
instructions, until al dente.
Tip into a colander and leave
to drain completely.

In a heavy-bottomed pan, make
the Starter Sauce, then reduce
the heat to low. Add all the
cheese and stir until melted.
Add the drained pasta to the
sauce and mix thoroughly.

Spread the corn chips over a
large serving plate. Spoon the
mac as evenly as possible over
the top, followed by the chilli.
Add the guac, salsa, jalapeños
and soured cream – the idea is
to create layers of flavour over
the chips.

Garnish with the coriander
leaves and serve to your hungry
crew with the lime wedges on
the side.

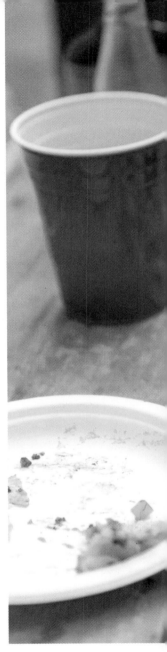

HOT CHICK

HEY FRANK! YOU'RE ONE HELLUVA GUY!

olive oil, for frying
6 skinless chicken thighs,
  cut into thin pieces
90g unsalted butter
1 garlic clove, minced
100ml Frank's RedHot Original
  Pepper Sauce
400g macaroni
1 x portion Starter Sauce
  (page 21)
100g mature Cheddar, grated
80g Monterey Jack, grated
110g Bleu d'Auvergne, crumbled,
  plus 80g to serve
4 tbsp soured cream
1 tbsp finely chopped
  fresh chives
sea salt
2 sticks celery, cut in half and
  sliced lengthways, to serve

In a high-sided sauté pan heat
the oil over a medium heat, add
the chicken pieces and cook
until golden and a little crispy.

In another pan over a low heat,
melt the butter. Add the garlic
and fry gently for a couple of
minutes. Add the Frank's sauce,
a pinch of salt and mix together
well. Tip the cooked chicken
into the sauce and coat
thoroughly and leave on a low
heat, stirring occasionally.

Meanwhile, bring a large pan of
salted water to the boil and
cook the pasta according to
the pack instructions, until al
dente. Tip into a colander and
leave to drain completely.

In a heavy-bottomed pan, make
the Starter Sauce, then reduce
the heat to low. Add the
Cheddar, Monterey Jack and 110g
of the Bleu d'Auvergne, and stir
until melted. Add the drained
pasta to the sauce and mix
thoroughly.

Spoon your mac into 4 bowls and
top each one with the chicken
and the remaining blue cheese.
Add a dollop of soured cream,
two pieces of celery and a
flourish of chopped chives to
each bowl and you're done.

LL COW J

THIS IS HARDCORE – BONE MARROW IN THE SAUCE?! HELL YEAH.

1 marrowbone, cut in half
   lengthways
1 tbsp unsalted butter
70g Japanese panko breadcrumbs
400g macaroni
1 x portion Starter Sauce
   (page 21)
150g mild Cheddar, grated
150g Ogleshield cheese, cubed
sea salt and freshly ground
   black pepper
a few sprigs of thyme, leaves
   finely chopped

Preheat the oven to 220°C/200°C (fan)/gas 7.

Place the marrowbone cut side up on a foil-lined baking tray and season with salt and pepper. Roast for 15 minutes, or until the marrow has a soft, jelly-like consistency. Scoop out the marrow and set aside.

Melt the butter in a frying pan over a low heat and toss in the panko breadcrumbs to coat. Raise the heat to medium and toast the breadcrumbs until golden. Set aside.

Meanwhile, bring a large pan of salted water to the boil and cook the pasta according to the pack instructions, until al dente. Tip into a colander and leave to drain completely.

In a heavy-bottomed pan, make the Starter Sauce, then reduce the heat to low. Add all the cheese and stir until melted, then add the marrow and mix thoroughly. Stir in the drained pasta.

Transfer the mac to 4 serving bowls, scatter the panko breadcrumbs and thyme over the top and season with salt and pepper.

TRAILER PARK PIE

TONY HAS A THING FOR A GOOD COTTAGE PIE; ANNA NOT SO MUCH. TO REACH A COMPROMISE THE TRAILER PARK PIE WAS BORN. WE USE SMOKED CHEDDAR IN THE MAC TO REPLICATE THE SMOKINESS OF A TRADITIONAL CHILLI COOKED OVER A FIRE.

Serves 8

1 x portion House Chilli
  (page 119)
400g macaroni
1 x portion Starter Sauce
  (page 21)
230g smoked Cheddar, grated
190g Monterey Jack, grated
30g Parmesan, grated
½ tsp smoked paprika

Preheat the grill to 220°C/200°C (fan)/gas 7.

Pre-prepare your chilli and while it's cooking, bring a large pan of salted water to the boil and cook the pasta according to the pack instructions, until al dente. Tip into a colander and leave to drain completely.

In a heavy-bottomed pan, make the Starter Sauce, then reduce the heat to low. Add the Cheddar, 90g of the Monterey Jack and all the Parmesan, stirring until melted. Add the drained pasta to the sauce and mix thoroughly.

Fill the bottom of an ovenproof dish with chilli so that the base is completely covered, then carefully spoon over the mac 'n' cheese. Cover the top with the remaining Monterey Jack and grill for 10 minutes, or until melted. Sprinkle with smoked paprika. This is comfort food Anna Mae's-style.

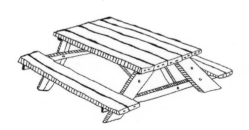

RIP SEBASTIAN

1 tbsp unsalted butter
70g Japanese panko breadcrumbs
1 whole lobster (about 600g)
400g macaroni
1 x portion Starter Sauce
  (page 21)
50g mature Cheddar, grated
100g Gruyère, grated
50g Fontina, grated
½ tsp Dijon mustard
½ tsp cayenne pepper
40g Parmesan, grated

Preheat the grill to 220°C/200°C
(fan)/gas 7.

Melt the butter in a frying pan
over a low heat and toss in
the panko breadcrumbs to coat.
Raise the heat to medium and
toast the breadcrumbs until
golden. Set aside.

Fill a large pan with enough
salted water so that your
lobster will be totally
submerged. Bring to the boil.
Plunge the lobster into the pot,
cover and cook for 8-10 minutes.
You'll know the lobster is good
to go when it is bright red and
if you pull at the antenna it
comes off with no resistance.
Remove the lobster and set it

aside to cool, then crack the
claws and shell and extract
the meat. Reserve the cooking
liquid.

Meanwhile, bring another large
pan of salted water to the boil
and cook the pasta according to
the pack instructions, until al
dente. Tip into a colander and
leave to drain completely.

In a heavy-bottomed pan, make
the Starter Sauce, then reduce
the heat to low. Add all the
cheese except the Parmesan and
stir with a wooden spoon until
melted, stirring occasionally
to stop the sauce sticking.

Add the lobster meat to the
cheese sauce along with a couple
of tablespoons of the reserved
cooking liquid, the mustard and
the cayenne pepper. Add the
pasta and stir to combine.

Transfer to a baking dish, cover
with the panko breadcrumbs,
sprinkle over the Parmesan and
grill for 10 minutes or until
golden and bubbling.

Our tribute to Sebastian from The Little Mermaid. He looks like a lobster by the way, Disney, not a bloody crab.

FUCK YOGA

GOAT'S CHEESE IS A SUPERFOOD.

olive oil, for frying
70g kale
400g macaroni
1 x portion Starter Sauce
  (page 21)
200g hard goat's cheese (e.g.
  goat's Gouda or St Helen's),
  grated
100g mild Cheddar, grated
70g walnuts, crushed
2 tbsp clear honey
4 sprigs of rosemary

Coat a frying pan with olive oil and heat over a medium flame. Add the kale and fry for 5 minutes, tossing occasionally to stop it burning. Set aside.

Bring a large pan of salted water to the boil and cook the pasta according to the pack instructions, until al dente. Tip into a colander and leave to drain completely.

In a heavy-bottomed pan, make the Starter Sauce, then reduce the heat to low. Add all the cheese and stir until melted. Make sure the heat is down low as goat's cheese has a tendency to split if heated too quickly. Add the drained pasta and kale to the sauce and mix together.

Transfer to 4 serving bowls, cover with the crushed walnuts, drizzle with the honey and finish with a sprig of rosemary.

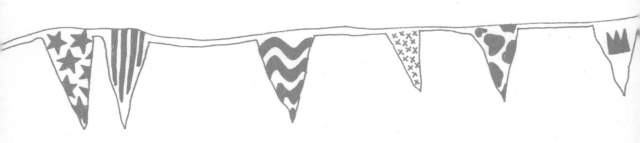

MACDMA

STINKY CHEESE IS OUR DRUG OF CHOICE.

400g macaroni
1 x portion Starter Sauce
  (page 21)
160g Munster*, rind removed and
  cheese cubed (you might want
  to wear gloves)
80g mild Cheddar, grated
80g Monterey Jack, grated

*or whatever cheese gets you
high

Bring a large pan of salted
water to the boil and cook the
pasta according to the pack
instructions, until al dente.
Tip into a colander and leave
to drain completely.

In a heavy-bottomed pan, make
the Starter Sauce, then reduce
the heat to low. Add all the
cheese and stir until melted.
Stir in the drained pasta.
Dish up. Tuck in. Trip out.
This is strong shit.

MAC 'N' SLEAZE

JACK IS OUR RESIDENT LOTHARIO. HE'S PERFECTED THIS BRUNCH MAC TO IMPRESS HIS DATES THE MORNING AFTER THE NIGHT BEFORE. DO AS JACK WOULD AND SERVE WITH A MIMOSA, FILTER COFFEE AND A WINNING SMILE.

Serves 2

200g macaroni
½ portion Starter Sauce
   (page 21)
115g mature Cheddar, grated
45g Monterey Jack, grated
¼ tsp English mustard
2 large pork sausages, skins
   removed
2 eggs

FOR THE HASH BROWNS
200g potatoes, peeled and grated
½ small onion, grated
15g unsalted butter, for frying
sea salt and freshly ground
   black pepper

Bring a large pan of salted water to the boil and cook the pasta according to the pack instructions, until al dente. Tip into a colander and leave to drain completely.

In a heavy-bottomed pan, make the Starter Sauce, then reduce the heat to low. Add all the cheese and the mustard, and stir until melted. Stir in the drained pasta. Keep over a low heat and stir occasionally to stop the mac sticking to the pan while you prepare the rest.

Now make your hash browns. Squeeze as much liquid as possible from the grated potatoes and tip into a bowl. Add the onions and season with salt and pepper. Squish into 2 hash-brown-shaped circles around 2cm thick.

Melt the butter in a non-stick frying pan over a medium-low heat. Add the hash browns and press them down firmly into the bottom of the pan with a spatula. Cook for 6-7 minutes each side, or until they are golden brown.

While the hash browns are cooking, press the sausage meat into 2 round patty shapes. Fry them over a medium heat in a large non-stick frying pan until cooked through, around 6 minutes. A minute or two before they've finished cooking, crack the eggs into the frying pan and cook until the whites are done and the yolks still runny.

Set out 2 plates, place a hash brown on each one and stack with the mac 'n' cheese, a sausage patty, and an egg. Serve, eat, usher guest out, get back on Tinder.

MACOLOGY

GETTING EXPERIMENTAL

THE QUICK ONE

**THIS A GREAT RECIPE WHEN YOU'RE
SHORT ON TIME AS IT CUTS OUT THE
STARTER SAUCE AND, LET'S FACE IT,
EVERYONE LOVES A QUICKIE.**

400g macaroni
400ml milk
½ tsp English mustard
280g mature Cheddar, pre-grated*
100g Monterey Jack, pre-grated*
30g mozzarella, pre-grated*
a pinch of salt

*buy pre-grated as the starch
used helps to thicken the sauce

Bring a large pan of salted
water to the boil and cook the
pasta according to the pack
instructions, until al dente.
Tip into a colander and drain
thoroughly, leaving the heat on.

Tip the pasta back into the pan,
add the milk and bring it to the
boil, then immediately turn the
heat down to medium. Stir
through the mustard and mix in
the cheese until melted. Season
with salt.

Smug face.

MAC NO CHEESE

**WE ALL THOUGHT WE KNEW OUR CREW
MEMBER SARA UNTIL SHE SUGGESTED
THIS NO CHEESE DISH...**

**BIG IN SWEDEN, SARA'S NATIVE LAND,
THIS WORKS REALLY WELL AS A SIDE DISH
TO A HEARTY, MEATY MAIN SUCH AS
MEATBALLS OR A RICH STEW.**

1 litre whole milk
1 tbsp unsalted butter
300g macaroni
a pinch of salt
a pinch of pepper
a pinch of grated nutmeg

In a large pan over a medium-
high heat, bring the milk and
butter to just under a boil.
Turn the heat down to medium-low
and add the uncooked pasta,
salt, pepper and nutmeg. Cook
for around 15 minutes, or
until the milk has virtually
evaporated, the pasta is cooked
and you have a creamy, thick pot
of steaming mac. Be sure to stir
the mac every few minutes to
stop it sticking to the pan.

MAC 'N' CHEESE FRIES

GENIUS!

YOU'LL NEED
a cooking thermometer

about 500g chilled leftover mac
  'n' cheese that's been
  refrigerated in a square
  container
500ml vegetable oil, for
  deep-frying
200g Japanese panko breadcrumbs
100g Parmesan, finely grated
1 egg, beaten
sea salt

Carefully transfer the mac from
its container on to a chopping
board; it should look like a
firm block. Slice the mac into
1cm-thick slices, then again
into lengths around 1cm wide.
You want to end up with sticks
around 1cm square and 7cm long.

Put the oil in a deep-sided
heavy-bottomed pan and heat
to 190°C. Combine the panko
breadcrumbs and the Parmesan
in a shallow dish.

Take each of your mac sticks
and roll it first in the beaten
egg and then in the Parmesan
breadcrumbs. Deep-fry in small
batches until golden, and then
drain on kitchen paper.

Sprinkle with salt and serve
with your fave dipping sauce.

SUPERFRY SNACK MAC

COULDN'T FINISH THAT MAC 'N' CHEESE FROM LAST NIGHT'S DINNER? FEAR NOT, FRY THE BEJEEZUS OUT OF IT AND IT BECOMES A DELICIOUS SNACK.

Makes about 10 balls

YOU'LL NEED
a cooking thermometer

about 500g chilled leftover
  mac 'n' cheese (must have
  been refrigerated)
50g pre-grated mozzarella
1 egg, beaten
300g plain flour, seasoned
  with salt and pepper
500ml vegetable oil, for
  deep-frying
1/2 tsp smoked paprika
Porno Pepper Sauce (page 112)

Take a 40-50g piece of cold mac and shape into a ball, slightly pushing your thumb into the centre to make a hollow. Grab a pinch of mozzarella and fill the thumbprint. Push the sides of the ball together, covering the mozzarella filling. Mould into a ball shape and repeat with the rest of the mac.

Roll each ball in the beaten egg, then in the flour so that they're fully coated.

Put the oil in a deep-sided, heavy-bottomed pan and heat to 190°C. Using a large metal slotted spoon, gently lower the balls into the hot oil. Fry for 5-6 minutes, or until golden brown. Remove from the pan and place on some kitchen paper to soak up the excess oil.

Sprinkle with paprika and serve with Porno Pepper Sauce, for dipping.

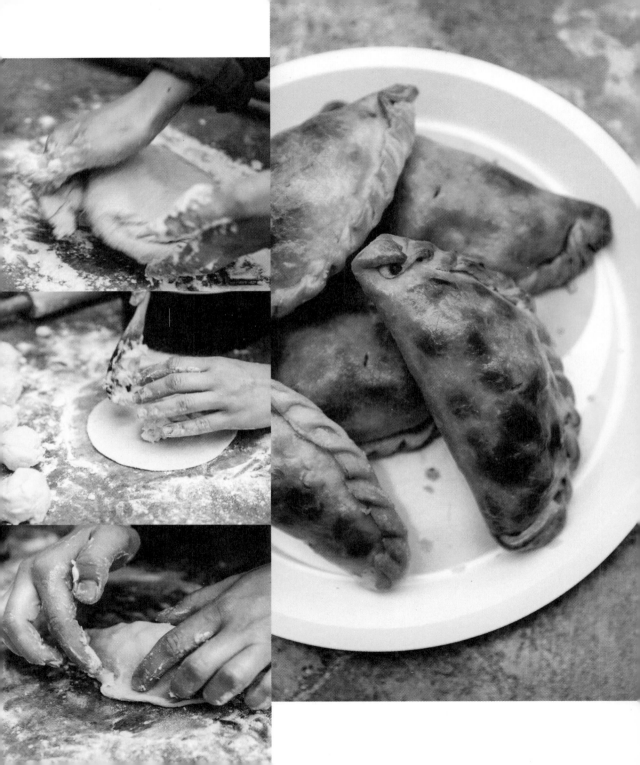

PASTA PAT'S EMPANADAS

MISTRESS OF MAC, PAZ IS ARGENTINIAN. WHEN SHE'S NOT MOANING THAT NO ONE UNDERSTANDS HER NAME (BAZ? PAT?), SHE'S ALWAYS BANGING ON ABOUT HOW YOU CAN'T FIND A GOOD STEAK IN LONDON. WE'RE INCLUDING HER OWN EMPANADA RECIPE HERE TO TRY AND PUT A SMILE ON THAT MOODY COW'S FACE.

Makes around 8 empanadas

about 16 tbsp leftover mac 'n' cheese
70g Monterey jack, grated
80g cooked prosciutto, roughly cut into 1.5cm squares
3 green jalapeño chillies, seeded and finely sliced

FOR THE EMPANADA DOUGH
300g plain flour, plus a little more for rolling
1½ tsp salt
115g lard, cubed
80ml cold water
1½ tbsp distilled white vinegar
2 eggs

First make the dough. Tip the flour, salt and lard into a big bowl and use your fingers to rub together until the mixture resembles large breadcrumbs.

Put the water, vinegar and 1 of the eggs into a second bowl and beat together with a fork. Add the flour mixture and stir gently to combine. The mixture will look pretty lumpy.

Tip the pastry on to a lightly floured surface and knead gently with the heel of your hand until it resembles a cohesive dough. Shape into a ball, wrap in cling film and refrigerate for 1 hour.

Preheat the oven to 200°C/180°C (fan)/gas 6.

Take the dough from the fridge and roll out on a lightly floured surface until it's about 5mm thick. Cut out 8 10cm-wide circles from the dough. Place 1 or 2 tablespoons of mac into the centre of each circle along with a sprinkling of cheese, ham and jalapeño. Fold the circle into a half-moon shape and pinch the edges closed with your fingertips.

Place the empanadas on a baking sheet lined with greaseproof paper. Beat the remaining egg and brush it over the tops. Bake for 25 minutes, or until golden brown. Crack a smile.

THE SMOKE CHOKE SOURDOUGH PRESS

TAKE THIS TO THE NEXT LEVEL AND ADD WHATEVER FILLINGS DO IT FOR YOU; HERE WE'VE USED OUR FAVOURITES.

Serves 1

2 tbsp salted butter, at room
 temperature
½ tsp lemon juice
2 slices good-quality sourdough
 bread
4 slices Monterey Jack
4 slices gruyère
2 slices thinly cut smoked
 chicken breast
3 halves chargrilled artichoke
 antipasto, sliced
80g chilled leftover mac
 'n' cheese*

*You can make your mac 'n'
cheese from scratch for this
recipe or use whatever you
have left over.

Combine the butter and lemon juice and spread the mixture over both sides of the bread slices. Arrange half the cheese slices over one slice of bread, then the chicken, the artichokes, the mac 'n' cheese and then the remaining slices of cheese. Try not to mound the ingredients, keep them evenly spread. Place the second slice of bread on top, in order to create a sandwich.

Heat both a frying pan and a heavy-bottomed pan over a medium heat. Transfer the sandwich to the frying pan and cook for a couple of minutes. Carefully turn the sandwich over and place the heavy-bottomed pan on top, squishing the sandwich together, for a further few minutes. Be careful not to let the sandwich burn. Remove from the heat when both sides are golden and the middle is nice and gooey. Cut in half and serve.

Bread and cheese; the backbone of civilisation.

MAC-PACKED PEPPERS

SO '70S, BUT SO GOOD.

200g macaroni
½ x portion Starter Sauce
  (page 21)
115g mature Cheddar, grated
50g Asiago cheese, grated
30g Parmesan, grated
3 tbsp fresh oregano leaves,
  roughly chopped
4 red bell peppers (choose ones
  that can stand on their base)
olive oil
4 thick slices of good-quality
  mozzarella
4 sprigs of basil

Preheat the oven to 200°C/180°C
(fan)/gas 6.

Bring a large pan of salted
water to the boil and cook the
pasta according to the pack
instructions, until al dente.
Tip into a colander and leave
to drain completely.

In a heavy-bottomed pan, make
the Starter Sauce, then reduce
the heat to low. Add all the
cheese and stir until melted.
Add the drained pasta and
chopped oregano to the sauce
and mix thoroughly.

Meanwhile, cut the tops off the
peppers and remove the seeds
with a spoon. Transfer to a
baking dish and rub generously
with olive oil. Spoon the mac
evenly into each pepper, top
with a slice of mozzarella and
drizzle with olive oil. Bake for
half an hour.

Serve with a sprig of basil on
each pepper.

WAFFLE MAC

SOMETHING YOU MIGHT TRY MAKING
AFTER A BIG NIGHT OUT, LIKE THE
LOADED PEANUT BUTTER, BANANA AND
DAIRY MILK TOASTED SANDWICH THAT
YOU CAN'T REMEMBER EATING AFTER
6 TEQUILAS AND A JÄGERBOMB.
PREMAKE THE MAC AND LEAVE IT TO
COOL READY FOR WAFFLING ON
YOUR RETURN.

YOU'LL NEED
a loaf tin
a waffle iron

400g macaroni
1 tbsp butter, for greasing
1 x portion Starter Sauce
  (page 21)
380g mature Cheddar, grated
240g Monterey Jack, grated
30g Parmesan, grated
8 rashers streaky bacon, cut
  into pieces
maple syrup, for drizzling

Bring a large pan of salted
water to the boil and cook the
pasta according to the pack
instructions, until al dente.
Tip into a colander and leave
to drain completely.

Butter your loaf tin.

In a heavy-bottomed pan, make
the Starter Sauce, then reduce
the heat to low. Add 230g of
the Cheddar, 90g of the Monterey
Jack and all the Parmesan
and mix thoroughly, stirring
occasionally to stop your sauce
sticking to the pan. Stir in
the drained pasta and spoon
the mixture into the buttered
loaf tin. Pop into the fridge
until cold.

Heat and butter your waffle
iron. Cut the cold mac loaf into
2.5cm slices. Take a slice and
sprinkle it with a mixture of
the remaining cheeses, then
lay another slice on top. Place
your mac sandwiches into the
hot waffle iron and cook until
golden brown. Repeat with the
rest of the mac.

Meanwhile, in a frying pan over
a medium-high heat, cook the
rashers of bacon until crisp.

Transfer your waffles from the
iron on to a plate and place
crispy bacon bits over the top.
Drizzle with as much maple syrup
as you desire.

MAC BOY SLIM

**ARE YOU REALLY GOING TO BUY THIS
BOOK IF YOU'RE COUNTING THE CALS?
PROBABLY NOT.**

600g butternut squash, peeled
  and cubed
500ml chicken or vegetable stock
200ml skimmed milk
1 garlic clove, minced
400g wholewheat or gluten-free
  pasta
3 heaped tbsp low-fat cream
  cheese
150g Parmesan, grated
1 bunch chives, finely chopped
sea salt and freshly ground
  black pepper

Put the squash, stock, milk
and garlic in a pan over a high
heat and bring to the boil, then
turn the heat down to medium.
Cook for 15 minutes, or until
the squash is tender. Drain,
reserving some of the cooking
liquid. Blend the squash with
a few tablespoons of the cooking
liquid until you have a smooth
sauce.

Meanwhile, bring a large pan
of salted water to the boil
and cook the pasta according
to the pack instructions, until
al dente. Tip into a colander
and leave to drain completely.

Pour the squash sauce into a
pan over a low heat. Add the
cream cheese and Parmesan
and stir until melted. Add
the drained pasta to the sauce
and mix thoroughly.

Spoon your guilt-free mac 'n'
cheese into 4 bowls and sprinkle
with chives. Or just eat the
lot, it doesn't count, right?

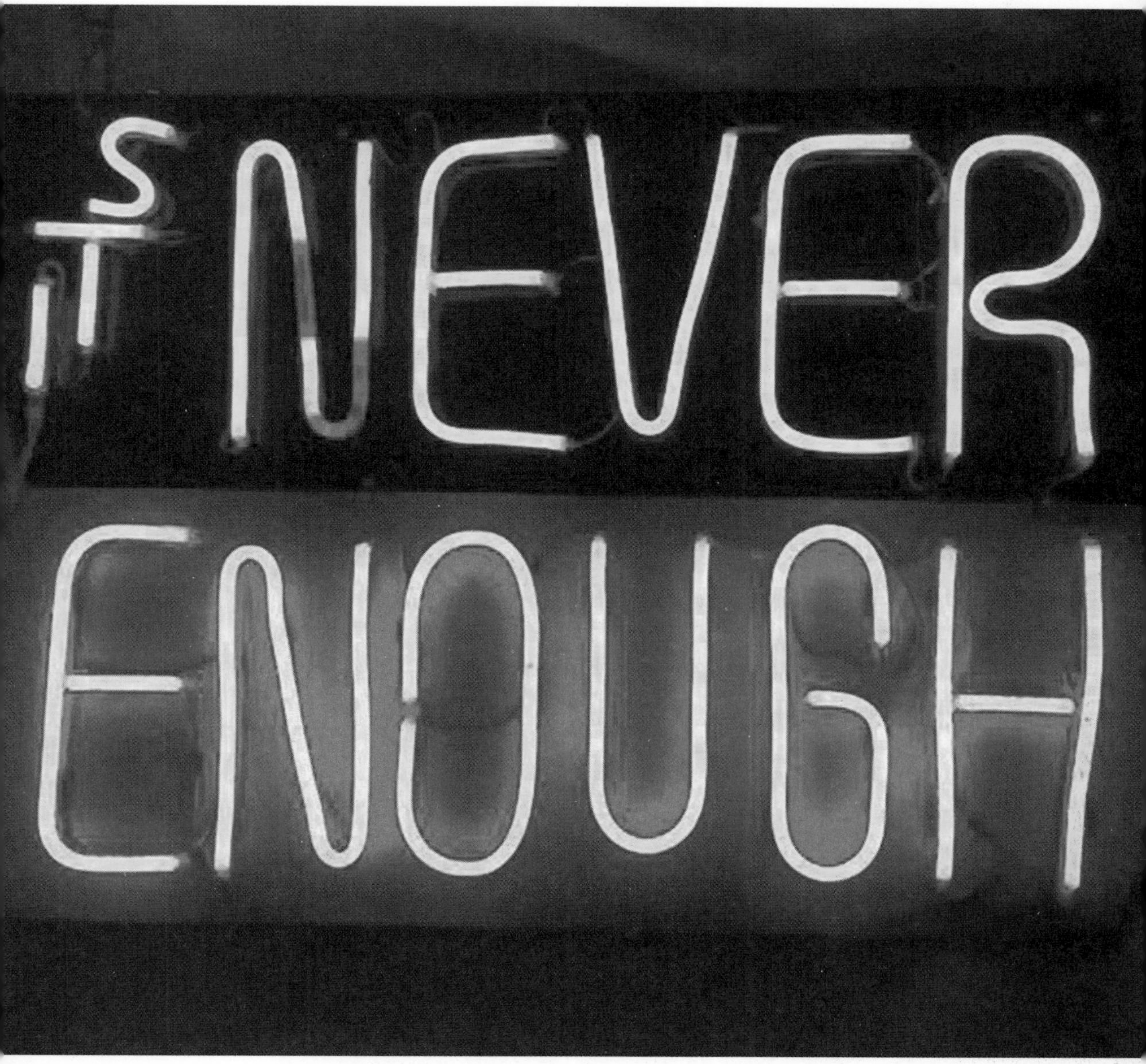

iTS NEVER
ENOUGH

BABY CHEESUS

IF WE COULD START THEM OFF IN THE WOMB, WE WOULD.

Makes 3-4 helpings

100g macaroni
1 tbsp frozen peas
50g mild Cheddar or other mild
  cheese, grated
2 tbsp low-fat cream cheese
1 tbsp sweetcorn

Bring a large pan of water
to the boil and cook the
pasta according to the pack
instructions, until soft, adding
the peas to the water for the
last 5 minutes. Tip into a
colander and leave to drain
completely, then return to the
pan. Reduce the heat to low.
Add the Cheddar, cream cheese
and sweetcorn and stir until
heated through.

Pour into a baby-sized receptacle
and feed on a spoon while doing
that aeroplane thing.

SCOOBY MACS

OUR FRENCH BULLDOG ALBUS GOES NUTS FOR THESE. ANGUS, OUR HUMAN COMPANION, IS ALSO PARTIAL TO A NIBBLE.

300g wholewheat flour, plus
  extra for dusting
100g mild Cheddar, grated
100g Parmesan, grated
1 egg, beaten
150ml chicken stock
4 tbsp leftover mac 'n' cheese

Preheat the oven to 180°C/160°C
(fan)/gas 4.

Put the flour, cheeses, egg and
stock into a large bowl and mix
with a wooden spoon until you
have a smooth mixture, adding
a little water if it's too dry.
Add the mac and stir through,
breaking up the noodles so
that they are evenly spread
throughout the mixture.

Roll out the dough on a floured
surface and cut into dog snack-
sized shapes or squares. Bake
for 20 minutes, or until golden.

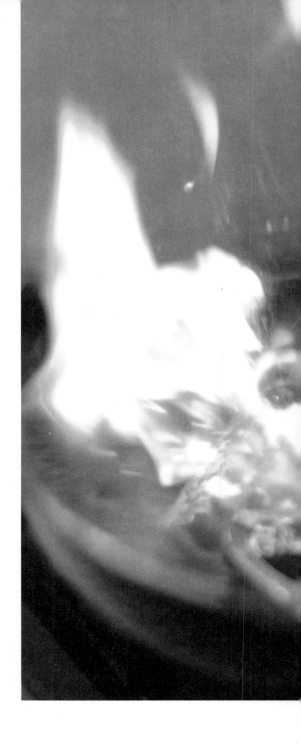

WINGMEN

GREAT COMPANY FOR MAC 'N' CHEESE

CHARRED PADRON PEPPERS

padrón peppers
oil, for frying
sea salt

Add some oil to a frying pan
and fry the peppers over a high
heat. Depending on the size of
the peppers they'll need about
7-9 minutes. You'll know they're
done when the flesh is soft and
the skin has large char marks
but aren't totally burnt.

KWIK KIMCHI

THIS CAN BE EATEN RIGHT AWAY, ALTHOUGH FOR THE TRUE EXPERIENCE IT SHOULD BE LEFT TO FERMENT FOR A FEW DAYS.

450g Chinese cabbage, cut into
   3cm-wide slices
50g carrots, thickly grated
2 spring onions, sliced
   lengthways
125ml cold water
2 tbsp salt
4 tbsp gochugaru paste (Korean
   chilli paste)
2 tbsp minced garlic
1 tbsp fish sauce
½ tbsp sugar
¼ tsp ginger powder

Put the cabbage, carrots, spring
onions, water and salt in a bowl
and give it a good stir to mix.
Leave for 10 minutes, then rinse
the salted veg in cold water a
few times, making sure the last
time that they're well drained.

In another bowl, mix together
all the rest of the ingredients
to make a paste.

Add the drained veg to the
paste and mix well.

Transfer to an airtight
container and store it in the
fridge for up to 2 weeks.

PICKLED REDS

THE SWEET AND SOUR OF THESE PICKLED ONIONS WORKS WITH ANYTHING CHEESY.

240ml white wine vinegar
50ml water
3 tbsp sugar
1 tsp salt
½ tsp mixed spice
4 cloves
1 bay leaf
4 tbsp freshly squeezed
  lime juice
2 medium red onions, sliced
  about 3mm thick

In a small pan over a low heat, warm the vinegar and water. Add the sugar, salt, mixed spice, cloves and bay leaf and stir for a couple of minutes, or until the sugar and salt have dissolved.

Stir in the lime juice, add the onions and transfer the mixture to an airtight container that just about holds the pickled onions. Leave to cool and refrigerate at least overnight and up to 2 weeks.

SPEEDY SAUERKRAUT

½ white onion, thinly sliced
½ white cabbage, thinly sliced
120ml beer
60ml cider vinegar
½ tbsp soft brown sugar
a pinch of mustard seeds
a pinch of caraway seeds
a pinch of salt

In a pan over a medium heat, lightly fry the onion for a few minutes, then add the cabbage and the rest of the ingredients. Bring up to a boil and then turn down the heat to a simmer and cook until the liquid has reduced by about half and the cabbage is tender.

Allow to cool, then serve or transfer to an airtight container and keep in the fridge for up to 2 weeks.

SALSA FRESCA

5 tomatoes, diced, seeds and
  jelly removed
2 green jalapeño chillies,
  seeded and diced
½ red onion, diced
a handful of coriander, chopped
a pinch of salt
juice of ½ a lime

Combine the tomatoes, jalapeños,
onion and coriander in a bowl,
season with the salt and mix
through the lime juice. Add
more lime if you dig the sour.
Refrigerate for a couple of
hours for the flavours to
combine before serving.

GUAC'

4 very ripe avocados
4 tbsp Salsa Fresca (see left)

Remove the skin and stones from
your avocados, keeping one stone
back. Mash the flesh into the
desired consistency, chunky or
smooth. Add the Salsa Fresca
and stir through. Eat as soon
as possible or, if making in
advance, add the stone to the
bowl to slow down the browning,
cover and refrigerate for up
to a day.

PORNO PEPPER SAUCE

XXX RATED.

YOU'LL NEED
a 500ml airtight glass bottle,
  sterilised*

about 30 hot fresh chilli
  peppers such as ghost,
  habanero or scotch bonnet,
  cut into 3mm slices
10 garlic cloves, crushed
10 black peppercorns
350ml water
450ml cider vinegar
vegetable oil, for frying

*to sterilise your bottle, first
preheat the oven to 140°C/120°C
(fan)/gas 1. Clean your bottle
in hot soapy water, rinse
thoroughly, then transfer to
the oven to dry completely.

Grease a sauté pan with
vegetable oil and fry the
chillies, garlic and peppercorns
over a medium heat for
3 minutes. Add the water and
continue to simmer for a
further 20 minutes, or until
the chillies are super soft
and the water has almost
evaporated. Open a window.

Turn the heat to low. Add the
vinegar and warm for about
5 minutes, then transfer to
a bowl or food processor and
blend thoroughly. Press the
mixture through a strainer
until you have a thin, smooth
sauce. Transfer to your bottle
and leave to mature in the
fridge for at least 5 days
when the sauce will be ready
to enjoy with everything.

LEMON-DRESSED SPINACH & FENNEL

150g baby spinach leaves
1 fennel bulb, finely sliced
a handful of sliced almonds

FOR THE DRESSING
4 tbsp olive oil
juice and rind of ½ a lemon
sea salt and freshly ground
  black pepper

In a small bowl, combine all
the dressing ingredients and
whisk together with a fork.
Put the spinach and fennel in
a salad bowl and drizzle over
the dressing. Cover the bowl
with a plate or similar and
toss until thoroughly combined.
Scatter with the sliced almonds
and serve.

AVO & BUTTER LETTUCE SALAD

2 heads of butter lettuce,
  leaves torn, rinsed and dried
1 avocado, sliced
¼ red onion, thinly sliced

FOR THE DRESSING
3½ tbsp olive oil
1½ tbsp red wine vinegar
½ tsp Dijon mustard
sea salt and freshly ground
  black pepper

In a small bowl, whisk together
the dressing ingredients. Put
the lettuce, avocado and onion
into another bowl and pour over
the dressing. Cover with a plate
and toss until fully dressed.

ROASTED BRUSSELS WITH BACON VINAIGRETTE

450g brussels sprouts, halved
3 tbsp olive oil
2 pinches of salt
4 slices dry-cured bacon,
  finely chopped

FOR THE DRESSING
5 tbsp balsamic vinegar
2 tsp brown sugar
1½ tsp Dijon mustard

Preheat the oven to 220°C/200°C (fan)/gas 7.

In a large bowl, toss the sprouts in the olive oil and salt. Transfer to a baking tray and roast for about 30 minutes, or until tender and charred.

Meanwhile, cook the bacon in a frying pan over a medium heat until crisp, reserving the fat.

In a bowl mix together the bacon fat, vinegar, sugar and mustard until combined. Pour over the sprouts, tossing them as you go. Top with the bacon and serve.

BACON, YOU MAKE EVERYTHING BETTER.

ZENA'S FRIED CAULIFLOWER & CHARD SALAD

1 cauliflower, cut into similar
  sized florets
4 tbsp olive oil
a pinch of salt
150g Swiss or rainbow chard,
  stemmed and chopped into
  ribbons
4 radishes, sliced into rounds
1 tsp yuzu citrus juice (yuzu
  is a type of Japanese citrus
  fruit)
2 tbsp honey
1 large red chilli pepper,
  seeded and sliced into rounds
2 tbsp toasted pine nuts

FOR THE DRESSING
3 tbsp olive oil
grated zest and juice of
  ½ a lemon
1 tsp chopped fresh dill

First prepare the cauliflower.
Bring a pan of water to the
boil and blanch the cauliflower
for 1-2 minutes, then drain
thoroughly. Transfer to a sauté
pan with the oil and fry until
golden brown and crispy. Season
with some salt and tip on to
kitchen paper. Leave to cool.

In a small bowl mix together the
olive oil, lemon zest and juice
and dill. Put the chard and
radishes in a large bowl and
drizzle over the lemon dressing.
Cover the bowl with a plate
or similar and toss until
thoroughly combined.

Lay the dressed chard on a salad
plate and layer the cauliflower
over the top. In another small
bowl, mix together the yuzu
juice and honey and drizzle this
over the cauliflower. Scatter
over the chilli slices and pine
nuts before serving.

HOUSE CHILLI

AVOID LEAN BEEF FOR THIS RECIPE AS THE FAT ADDS TO THE FLAVOUR. THE QUALITY OF THE MEAT REALLY DOES MAKE THIS DISH, SO GO FOR THE BEST YOU CAN.

2 onions, diced
1 red pepper, roughly chopped into medium chunks
1 green pepper, roughly chopped into small chunks
500g ground chuck steak (ask your butcher) or good-quality ground beef mince
300g puréed tomatoes
4 garlic cloves, minced
1 x 400g tin pinto or black-eye beans, drained
250ml beef stock
2 tbsp dried oregano
1 heaped tbsp ground cumin
1 tsp cayenne pepper
1 tsp ground black pepper
½ tsp smoked paprika
1 heaped tsp cocoa powder
3 tbsp cider vinegar
a slug of bourbon
2 tsp smoked chipotle Tabasco (or to taste)
a big pinch of salt
vegetable oil, for frying

Add a glug of oil to a large pan over a low heat and cook the onions and peppers for about 10 minutes, or until soft.

Turn up to a medium heat and add the beef to the onions and peppers, browning the meat all over. Add the puréed tomatoes, garlic, beans and stock and stir well. The pot should be simmering, not boiling.

Sprinkle in the oregano, spices, cocoa powder, cider vinegar and bourbon, followed by the Tabasco, and stir thoroughly. Cook over a low heat for about 20 minutes, or until the beef is tender, adding a little water if it looks like it's getting too dry. Taste for heat and salt before you serve and make any final adjustments.

SUGAR & SWIG

**MONEY CAN'T BUY HAPPINESS,
BUT IT CAN BUY ICE CREAM AND BOOZE.**

POP BITCH

**TASTES SWEET, BUT WILL GIVE YOU
A SLAP AROUND THE FACE.**

YOU'LL NEED
4 x ice-lolly moulds

1 whole watermelon, diced
4 green chillies, seeded and
  finely diced
juice of 2 limes
a pinch of salt
6 tbsp light agave syrup

Put all the ingredients except
the agave syrup into a blender
and blitz thoroughly until
smooth. Sweeten with the syrup
to taste. Pour into lolly moulds
and freeze.

DEEP-FRIED ICE CREAM

YOU'LL NEED
a cooking thermometer

4 large scoops of ice cream,
  your fave flavour
3 handfuls of frosted corn
  flakes
½ tsp ground cinnamon
a pinch of salt
2 eggs, beaten
1 litre vegetable oil,
  for deep-frying
hot chocolate sauce, to serve

Place the ice cream scoops on a
tray, cover them with cling film
and place in the freezer for
half an hour.

Put the corn flakes, cinnamon
and salt in a plastic bag and
crush into crumbs. Scatter over
a flat surface such as a
chopping board or wide plate.

Take the ice cream from the
freezer, remove the cling film
and roll them in the corn flake
crumbs until well coated. Put
them back on the tray and into
the freezer.

After 30 minutes take the balls
out of the freezer and roll in
the beaten egg, then cover in
a second coating of corn flake
crumbs. Pop back into the
freezer.

Just before serving, pour the
oil into a deep-sided pan so
that it's around three-quarters
full, and heat to 160°C. Remove
the balls from the freezer and
deep-fry until golden, around
30 seconds.

Serve immediately, with hot
chocolate sauce for a full-on
mouthgasm.

BUTTERMILK PANCAKES

POPULAR AT FESTIVALS WITH THE EARLY RISERS, OR ACTUALLY MAYBE THEY JUST HAVEN'T GONE TO BED YET ...

160g self-raising flour
2 tbsp golden caster sugar
¾ tsp baking powder
240ml buttermilk
1 egg
2 tbsp butter, melted
a pinch of salt
4 tbsp crème fraîche, to serve
200g freshly chopped fruit
  of your choice, to serve
icing sugar, to serve

Combine the flour, sugar and baking powder in a large bowl. In another bowl combine the buttermilk, egg and 1 tablespoon of the melted butter, and a pinch of salt. Gradually pour this mixture over the flour and whisk to a smooth batter.

Grease a non-stick frying pan over a medium heat with the remaining butter. Pour around half a ladleful of the batter into the pan so that you have a pancake about 10cm in diameter. When air holes develop on the top and edges start to form, flip the pancake and cook until golden brown, about 2 minutes each side. Repeat until all the batter is used up - you should get 8 pancakes.

To serve, stack two pancakes per person and top with a couple of tablespoons of crème fraîche and the fresh fruit and a dusting of icing sugar. Eat. Go to bed.

IN TRANSIT (1998, DIESEL)

THIS CIDER COCKTAIL IS ESSENTIAL TO THE ANNA MAE'S FESTIVAL SEASON. TRAVELLING AROUND THE COUNTRY ALLOWS US TO SAMPLE LOCAL SCRUMPIES AND OUR GANG HAVE BECOME QUITE THE CONNOISSEURS. FOR THE FULL EFFECT MIX THIS UP IN AN EMPTY SOFT-DRINK BOTTLE IN THE BACK OF A TRANSIT VAN, THEN DESIGNATE THE UNLUCKY PERSON WITH THE BACKPACK TO CARRY IT AROUND ALL NIGHT.

YOU'LL NEED
1 x 1 litre empty soft-drink
bottle

2 limes
150ml dark rum
a few shakes of Angostura
  bitters
470ml regional medium-dry
  flat cider
370ml ginger beer

Squeeze the juice of 1 of the limes into the empty bottle, finely slice the other lime and push it through the bottleneck. Pour in the rum, add a few shakes of bitters, the cider and then the ginger beer. Give it a swirl, being careful it doesn't fizz over the top.

STRAWBERRY HARSHMALLOW SHAKE

WHAT A WONDERFUL WAY TO USE UP LEFTOVER MILK.

32 marshmallows
1 litre whole milk
200ml white rum
4 scoops vanilla ice cream
4 scoops strawberry ice cream
32 strawberries, tops removed
  and cut into quarters

Preheat the grill to 180°C/160°C (fan)/gas 4.

Place the marshmallows on greaseproof paper and shove them under the grill until slightly melting and golden, a couple of minutes, max. Blend all the ingredients except for 8 of the melted marshmallows until smooth. Pour into 4 glasses and top with the remaining toasted mallows.

THE GREEN MAN

GREEN MAN FESTIVAL IS HELD IN THE BEAUTIFUL GREEN WELSH HILLS, WITH LOTS OF GREEN-WELLIED FOLK LISTENING TO CHILLED OUT MUSIC – IT MAKES US FEEL WHOLESOME... AND WELL, GREEN – JUST LIKE THIS SMOOTHIE.

1.2 litres cloudy apple juice
2 ripe mangos, stoned and cubed
juice of 2 limes
8 tbsp light agave nectar
200g baby kale, stalks removed
8 tbsp chopped fresh mint leaves

Blend all the ingredients until you have a smooth liquid. Add more apple juice if you prefer a thinner consistency. Neck the lot, feel great.

BLACK CHERRY MARGARITAS

150ml gold tequila
4 tbsp lime juice
1 jar black cherries in kirsch
275g ice
1 lime, thinly sliced

Mix the tequila and lime juice along with 6 tablespoons of kirsch from the jar of cherries. Add the ice and blend until smooth. Pop 2 cherries into the bottom of each of your glasses and pour over the blended marg. Garnish with 2 thin slices of lime and 1-2 cherries.

I EAT GLITTER FOR BREAKFAST

GG&T

ALL THINGS IN MODERATION. EXCEPT GLITTER AND GIN.

YOU'LL NEED
edible glitter
an ice-cube tray

200ml London dry gin, such
  as Portobello Star
600ml tonic water
1 lime, cut into quarters

Sprinkle a pinch of glitter into
each mould in your ice-cube tray
and carefully fill with water.
Freeze until solid.

Sprinkle some more glitter into
a shallow bowl. Take your glasses
and rub the rims with water,
then dip them in the bowl so
that the rims are glittery.

Crack out your glitter ice and
add some cubes to the glasses.
Pour over the gin, then
carefully add the tonic. Finish
with a piece of lime, a pinch
more glitter and a straw, you
sparkly bitch.

BUTTERED COFFEE

THIS ENERGY HIGH MIGHT BE LEGAL BUT WE CAN'T PROMISE YOU WON'T END UP A JITTERY MESS.

YOU'LL NEED
a milk frother

4 mugs freshly brewed
  good-quality hot coffee
100ml bourbon
4 tbsp unsalted butter
4 tsp soft brown sugar
4 tsp coconut oil

Pour all the ingredients into
a jug and stir until melted
and mixed. Give it a whizz
with your milk frother until
there's some foamy goodness.
Pour into 4 mugs.

A word about wine

There has been a massive explosion in the popularity of craft beer in the last few years, and we are not denying that beer and mac are perfect partners.

But being partial to the odd vino now and then, we got talking to our wine buddies Jackson Steel down in Peckham wine country who came up with some pairings that are pretty off the scale. People weren't having cheese and wine parties all over the show in the '70s for nuttin'…

#CHEESUSLOVESYOU
A Chardonnay. Something oak-aged & buttery from California or Burgundy.

THE SPICY JUAN
An Argentinian Malbec with a bold smokiness to punch back at the chilli.

MACLETTE
A dry, crisp Chenin Blanc.

HOT CHICK
A sweet Tokaji from Hungary to cut through the saltiness.

WE'VE HAD LOTS OF SUPPORT AND ADVICE FROM MANY PEOPLE, BUT SOME NEED A SPECIAL MENTION...

All our amazing helpers past and present - Pasta Patricia and Sole (for controlling her), Zena Ribena/Cortina/Ballerina, AnGoose the boy wonder, Jack The Swift, Edam Adam, Cookie Super Doodles and her amazing illustrations, Selfie Sara, Stefi, Cousin Eve, Cousin Jack, John (?!), 'elen Balloon, Crystal. All the traders who've ever lent us something/helped us out/given advice (the list is endless). Petra for the start back in the heady Eat St days, we probably wouldn't be here without you. The Kerb Krew - Millie, Ollie, Orphelia, Lianna, Rob - we promise never to be late again (though always ready on time!). Ms Marmite Lover for day one of street food slinging. Kate for our first ever mac 'n' cheese stall. Caroline and the fabulous markets team at Glasto. Hilary and MAMA Lulu for accepting us for our first ever festivals. Fran at Green Man. Hilary at Secret Garden. Lottie for involving us in some great events when we'd first started.

Dom and the crew at Street Feast. Rhiannon and Olly for the beautiful designs and festival stall. Jacob & Dan at Work+Play. Verity & Vivo for giving their support, love, time and enthusiasm always. The Sledge. Gary for introducing us to the LA food truck scene. Ritchie for always cheering us on. Cha Cha the truck doctor. Alfie Lips. Anna's therapist - no seriously. Anna's mum for Albus sitting. Our parents for all the support and always being positive. Fran, Fred, Philippa and Laura, and everyone at Square Peg for being so laid-back about the endless mood boards we sent through. Everyone else that's taken a punt on us, eaten with us and come back for more.

Cheesuslovesyou

INDEX